Donkey lived in a small town by the sea. His master was a young man with a long red beard.

Every day he took Donkey to the docks where the big ships were unloading.

Every day he loaded boxes on Donkey's back. The boxes were heavy and Donkey had to carry them to the market.

They walked slowly past the big ships. His master sang but Donkey could only just manage to carry his load.

The man with the red beard didn't notice that Donkey got tired. Each day the load seemed to get heavier.

Then one day Donkey's master bought a van. "I won't need you any more," he said, and he drove away.

At first, Donkey was pleased. "I won't need to carry any more boxes," he thought. Then he wondered who would feed him.

Perhaps he could find someone who would like a donkey. The postman didn't. He had a bicycle.

The policeman didn't. He had a fast police car.

Nobody wanted a donkey. Not even the farmer, he had a tractor.

Donkey wandered down on to the beach. He saw a crowd of children.

They were waiting to have a ride on a beautiful pony. But they had to wait so long they were getting cross.

"Come and help me," said the man on the beach. So Donkey helped and all the children had a ride.

They didn't mind that he wasn't beautiful like the pony. They all gathered round him and patted him and gave him something to eat.

When the sun disappeared behind the houses the man on the beach said to his pony, "We must go home now." But the pony wanted Donkey to go with them.

"All right, Donkey can come home too," said the man. Donkey saw the lights of the boats and thought, "I hope the van doesn't break down."